simple

stamps & stencils

style

simple

stamps & stencils

style

SACHA COHEN

Photographs by Lucinda Symons

M·Q·P

Acknowledgements

Thanks to Lucy Fanthorpe and Suzanne Carter for styling,
to Steve Gott and Jon Self for making up the sets
and to Joss O'Brien for assisting.

♥

Published by MQ Publications, Ltd.
254-258 Goswell Road, London EC1V 7EB

Copyright © MQ Publications, Ltd. 1998

Text and Designs © Sacha Cohen 1998

Series Editor: Ljiljana Ortolja-Baird
Editor: Jane Warren
Designer: Bet Ayer
Photographer: Lucinda Symons
Stylist: Diana Civil

A CIP catalogue record for this book is available from the British Library

ISBN: 1 897954 19 0

Printed in Italy

1 3 5 7 9 8 6 4 2

c o n t e n t s

introduction 6

introduction

♥

The creative urge exists in all of us. Perhaps denied expression by the more pragmatic activities of our hectic lifestyles, side-tracked by lack of confidence and tight budgets, or obscured by time, nevertheless, we have all known the thrill of making something beautiful. But for many of us, our efforts at primary school were the pinnacle of our creative success, and the thought of applying long-forgotten glueing, painting, cutting and drawing skills to the decoration of our homes merely inspires a phone call to that much-recommended, reputable (and reassuringly expensive) interior decorator.

It need not be so. Even the least 'crafty' among us can achieve stylish decor, using the simple techniques of stencilling and stamping. With these techniques, as with our earliest creations, the accent is on individuality and freedom of expression. No right and wrong, but a whole world of possibilities in between. Just as your wardrobe, photo album and garden differ from everyone else's, so should the décor of your home, reflecting the tastes and personalities within. The joy of stencilling and stamping is knowing that your creations are unique, and no amount of catalogue browsing will allow their duplication.

Simple Style Stamps & Stencils introduces the novice to projects which are simple, both in their design and their execution. Each is well within the capabilities of the average person, and the materials required are the sort that we all have ready access to: paint, brushes, masking tape and the like. The reader already familiar with the art of stencilling and stamping will find these pages brimming with fresh ideas sure to rekindle his or her enthusiasm.

As with other elements of simple style, in the use of stencilling and stamping, less is definitely more. There is nothing worse than the overkill of every spare surface and object boasting some embellishment. A light touch is essential here. Used with restraint, simple stencilled designs will enhance the tranquillity of the home, whereas a riot of designs will compete with each other to clutter the visual space. On any particular piece, if the question arises 'Should I repeat the design again – or add another?', the answer should be 'no'. It is better to err on the side of subtlety, and you can always add to the design later, if you feel the urge!

Stencilling and stamping have been used as an art form for many centuries. The Egyptians were using stencil art to embellish their mummy cases as long ago as BC2500, but it may have been the Chinese who first adopted the concept of using repeating patterns, as early as BC3000. Since the earliest forms of stencils were fashioned from perishable materials, including leaves, bark and skin, the exact origins of the process are obscure. Fiji islanders traditionally used bamboo and banana leaves for their stencils; the Inuit people of Baffin Island used dried sealskin; while in the Far East, varnished mulberry fibre produced a more durable stencil, excellent for printing on fabric. In Japan, stencilled silk had become highly sought-after by 600AD, but even the poorest folk employed the technique to decorate their cotton clothing and, by the 11th century, even Samurai armour boasted intricate stencilled patterns. With the spread of this art via the silk and spice trade routes, stencilling was absorbed by the culture of each adoptive country. Thus Thai stencils reflected largely the local flora and fauna, Indian patterns favoured geometric designs and the superb Persian designs depicted tales sacred to their culture. With the dawn of printing in 15th-century Europe, stencils were used to add colour to woodcut illustrations and in the production of playing cards. Block printed (stamped) fabric was first imported from India into Europe in the mid 1600s. Early, formalised flower patterns in the subdued hues afforded by plant dyes (mainly *madder*), were later vitalised by the advent of blue and yellow dyes. Stencilling reached a peak in Europe in the 19th century, when the technique was employed to decorate wallpaper, walls, fabric and furniture. In the New World, nostalgic settlers embellished the walls, furniture – and especially floorcloths – of their homes using remembered patterns from the Motherland. Perhaps the first interior designers were the travelling artisans who trundled about New England with their brushes, pigments and stencils, plying a new trade in home decorating!

▶ 7

In Britain, stencilling is among many paint techniques now enjoying a revival. When the Art Nouveau designs of Charles Rennie Mackintosh burst upon the scene at the end of the 1900s, (having been commissioned for that famous Glasgow meeting place Miss Cranston's Rose Tree Tea Rooms), the ancient art of stencilling was delivered, fit and well, into the glare of the 20th century.

This book is divided into five chapters, each of which focuses on a potential 'canvas' for your stencilling and stamping creativity: fabric, furniture, walls, floor and accessories. The projects within each chapter have been chosen for their simplicity and adaptability. Bearing in mind the elements of simple style – function and style – and applying personal tastes and colour schemes, the reader can adapt any of these projects to suit their own environment. The ideas shown here may be mixed and matched, applied to a different object in a different setting, or merely used as the creative spark to initiate other original project ideas – the possibilities are limited only by the imagination.

Every room of the house can benefit from the judicious use of stencilling. In the kitchen, the lettering and labels idea is perfect for sorting out your food storage jars, and either of the chequerboard designs make a cheerful – and practical – floor treatment. The striking monogram project is a great way to personalise a hallway or formal dining room; the tulip wall frame, quite attractive enough to stand alone, makes more of a wall sconce or treasured painting, and the bathroom is the perfect setting for our fresh, mosaic tile-effect table and nautical floor design. The sanc-tuary of the bedroom is enhanced by delicate designs and calm colour schemes, epitomised here by the ice poppy linen and feather-motif curtains.

We probably all own items of furniture which could do with a 'face lift', and there is something particularly pleasing about turning a drab and neglected piece into something really special. The chest of drawers, blanket box and chair projects featured give you the simple means to do just that.

Each project has been specially chosen or designed with speed and a limited budget in mind. Even the most complex projects, such as the checked stamped floor, table linen and blanket box are well within the scope of a weekend's work, while applying the stencilled or stamped designs to the curtains and bed linen took no more than a couple of hours.

The art of stencilling and stamping is an easy, effective and rapid way of personalising and beautifying your home; best of all, it's fun!

INTRODUCTION

floors

▶ 11

The downtrodden floor – often disregarded in our enthusiasm for choosing the colours, fabrics and furnishings for a room – is nonetheless a vital element in the decorative scheme of things. From the understated wall-to-wall carpet in neutral tones through rustic or high-tech tiles and vibrant scatter rugs to the warm honey tones of varnished floorboards, the floor is a potential source of both visual quietude and stimulation. It provides visual continuity between rooms in an open plan home and is often the link which allows an eclectic mix of styles in a room to work successfully. Unfortunately, the other characteristic of all floors is their uncanny affinity for dust, mud, and food spills and, in high-traffic areas, particularly in homes with young children, the visual link between rooms may at times be provided by a trail of unwelcome mud! For this reason, practicality is a high priority when it comes to choosing a floor finish.

Wooden floors are my personal favourite; I love the texture, grain and warmth of the wood, and, best of all, they are very easy to keep clean. Wooden floors are also versatile, and, given the right attention, can be used in virtually any part of the home. They can be sealed or varnished, painted. stained or lime washed and, of course, they make a wonderful 'canvas' for stencilling and stamping designs. With floors, you can be quite bold with the colour and scale of your design – the size of the area is quite liberating – but avoid too many 'repeats' and steer clear of fussy designs. A border

stencil is often all you need to transform the room, and it may be wise to first sketch your design on a floor plan before you begin. Other than that, stencilling or stamping floors couldn't be easier, as you will see from the four suggested projects in this chapter: a cool green 'gingham' floor; a floor stamped in colourful checks; a lime washed floor with drifts of autumn leaves and a bathroom floor given a fresh, nautical look.

FLOORS

checked stamped floor

♥

Painting wooden floor boards is the simplest way of decorating a floor. You can choose from a huge range of colours and, when you decide to redecorate the room, you can simply repaint the floor for a very modest outlay. From a practical point of view, the painted floor is hard to beat; a soft broom and a wet mop are all you need to keep it clean and, of course, a new coat of paint will refresh the floor at any time.

If you would like something a bit more decorative, then using a stamp to create a pattern on your floor couldn't be easier. For this floor, I have used simple square stamps to apply an unusual combination of yellow/cream and lilac/mauve to achieve an overall checked effect. A plain yellow rug complements the floor pattern beautifully.

▶ 15

Left: Detail of the colourful
stamped floor.

leaf stamped
lime floor

♥

Bring the outdoors in with a seasonal theme – this unusual floor finish is an ideal choice for a room or conservatory that overlooks the garden or where uncarpeted areas are the most practical solution.

Bare floorboards need not be dull, as this unusual stamped border shows. In this project, which involves first stamping on the design and then coating the floor with a lime wash, you have the chance to be creative with matt and gloss finishes, contrasting one against the other to highlight the natural grain and finish of the wood.

Natural images are uncomplicated and restful to the eye – their use suggests a warmth of colour and complements neutral shades in a room.

18 ◄

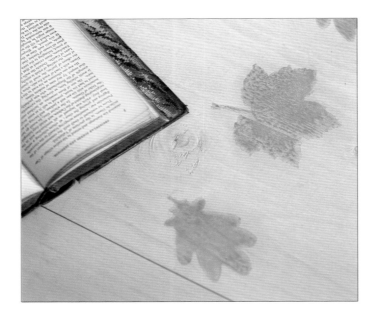

Close-up showing two leaf print details.

green
gingham floor

♥

We have gingham curtains, gingham table cloths, gingham chair covers – why not then, a gingham floor? The characteristic elements of gingham are perfect for a wooden floor: the repeating, regular pattern of squares; the simple white base colour teamed with green; the freshness, simplicity and the practicality of the design. Once I'd determined to make a gingham floor, I couldn't wait to get started.

Creating the gingham design involves three easy stages. The width of the floorboards determines the size of the checks, and the floorboards themselves provide a convenient straight edge. Stripes in green are stippled first in one direction, and then the other (at 90° to the first). Lastly, the intersections of the stripes are emphasised using a square stencil and a darker shade of green. Of course, you could choose to use two different colours, to create a 'tartan' effect, but bear in mind the unavoidable combination of colours at the intersections.

Detail showing mottled effect of stamps.

FLOORS

nautical rope twist floor

♥

Choose a fresh colour scheme for your bathroom, where cleanliness is a top priority. Blues and greens and maritime themes – especially fish and shell motifs – are popular for obvious reasons, but there is enormous scope for individuality here. In fact, the ceramic and glass world of baths, showers and basins can be a lifeless one, crying out for colour, focus and interest. If you have been wondering where to hang a quirky print, or where to display that unique first attempt at a ceramic 'bowl', then look no further, for if there is one room in the home which can accommodate a sense of humour, it is the bathroom.

I have given this floor a nautical look with a border stencil in a rope twist design. The stencil is not painted in solid colour, but rather gently stippled along its edge, to create the impression of shading and the desired three-dimensional effect.

▶ 23

Close-up showing the shading effect of stencilling.

walls

The choice of wall treatments and finishes is almost infinite. Apart from the standard coat of paint, there are thousands of wallpaper designs to choose from, as well as the options of using fabric or wood panelling, in order to achieve your desired effect. If, like me, the thought of wallpapering a room brings back uncomfortable memories of earlier attempts when the initial enthusiasm was rapidly replaced by frustration, don't despair. You need not be confined to a lack-lustre world dominated by jaded creams and off-whites; instead, you can introduce colour and life into your rooms using simple paint techniques, stamps and stencils.

Before painting, first determine the effect you want to achieve. This will depend on the function of the room. A formal sitting room will have different requirements from a child's playroom or the guest bedroom. Do you want the room to have a calm, restrained atmosphere, or is the accent on fun and spontaneity? Next, make a note of those features of the room itself which you might like to accentuate, such as an alcove, or an unusual window.

In most rooms, the walls act as a foil for the other decorative elements of the room: the curtains, furniture and accessories. In this case, a subtle paint effect or simple stencilled design work best. In other rooms, the decorative treatment of the walls is integral to the theme of the room. Children's rooms, for example, come alive with stencilled characters from favourite tales, while a row of stencilled botanical 'framed prints' in a bathroom make a practical alternative to pictures obscured behind misted-up glass.

In this chapter, I have chosen four different projects to illustrate the diversity of stencilling and stamping: an illumination-style monogram; a cool white-on-blue spiral design; a picture panel with a two-colour tulip design and a unique wall finish which I discovered, quite literally, by accident.

s p i r a l
w a l l   f i n i s h

♥

The quiet elegance of a restrained colour scheme appealed to my desire for a restful and calm interior when I made my first outline sketch for this room. A cool matt blue mottled background offset with a crisp white stencil effectively creates an atmosphere of peace and tranquillity.

The symmetry of a repeating curling scroll and rosette motif lends a classical appearance, adding focus and interest to the wall without jarring. This understated style blends into the background, providing the canvas against which the furniture and soft furnishings are allowed to become the focus of attention.

The scroll pattern appears like a rosette when viewed close up.

plaster spot
wall finish

♥

As with many things in life, an accident can be the beginning of a new and successful idea. This was indeed the case with this project. The handle of my paint roller fell into the tub of drying plaster. Having wiped off the plaster, I stood the roller on its end on newspaper to dry, unaware that the handle had a half-inch indentation in which the plaster had settled. Some hours later, I removed the roller from the newspaper. The plaster in the handle had slid onto the paper and dried, leaving a perfect circle. This technique can be applied to any surface and is a good solution when a very discreet finish is required.

An end of a small roller is a perfect stamp and the handle provides adequate pressure to emboss the mixture.

initial letter
monogram
♥

The art of illumination – the practice of adorning text with intricate illustrations which tease the eye, then reveal the capital letter at the beginning of a chapter – has always held a fascination for me. Perhaps the special appeal of this ancient art is the unique combination of consummate skill and attention to detail, the vibrant palette and the extravagant, often fanciful, interpretation of a single letter.

This design for an initial monogram, although much simplified, was inspired by the art of illumination. Stencilled in two colours, the letter and frame design has a three-dimensional look, and the details picked out in gold lend a sophisticated touch. The design looks dramatic against a backdrop of a strong base colour, as here. When you have finished this most unusual way of personalising your walls, just sit back, relax – and wait for a guest to ask you the name of your decorator!

Two stencils were used to create this design – a solid background overlaid with colourful details.

t u l i p
w a l l   p a n e l

♥

Make more of a treasured antique wall sconce or a painting by creating this unusual frame. Alternatively, in the right setting, this design is strong enough to stand alone: you could coax an awkward alcove from the shadows with this kind of attention, or you could try repeating the panel along a wall in a very large room for dramatic effect.

In each instance, it is important to first consider the proportions of the panel in relation to the wall and the room, and then scale the design up or down as appropriate. Also, it is advisable to carefully mark out the panel using a spirit level before you begin painting, to avoid disappointment later on.

Close-up showing tulip detail.

fabric

▶ 39

Over many centuries, fabric has been stencilled and stamped for use as window dressings, wallhangings, clothing and floorcloths. The wide range of fabric available to us today only serves to increase the possibilities.

Most fabric will accept a stencil, but, for the beginner, there are a few things to bear in mind when choosing cloth. For clear results, choose fabric which is closely woven, without a glaze (like chintz), and without surface texture. However, for those keen to experiment, textured fabrics can create unusual broken patterns in the stencil design. Expensive does not necessarily equal best, and inexpensive, natural fabrics such as calico, cambric, denim,

curtain lining and muslin, are all stamp work. In fact, it is always colour combinations on scrap fab- fabrics are best; a stencil design Even floor coverings can be sten- England floorcloth is the most colourful floorcloth effect may be a tear, spills and ills of high-traffic suitable base for stencilling or

excellent bases for stencil and wise to practise techniques and ric first. In general, self-coloured will be lost on a patterned fabric. cilled successfully. The New obvious example and creating a cunning disguise for the wear and zones. Carpets with a pile are not a stamping.

In this chapter, I have chosen four projects which are striking, yet surprisingly simple to make: a natural linen table setting, stamped and stencilled with a sea-shell motif; fresh Egyptian cotton bed linen delicately sprinkled with ice poppies; a sumptuous velvet cushion, stencilled and braided and curtains with a feather-light design in a contrasting colour.

These projects rely on colour contrasts and simple designs for their dramatic effects. Remember that the colour of the base fabric may affect the colour used for the stencil, so, to avoid disappointment, be sure to test your colour combination out on a scrap of fabric before you begin.

FABRIC

feather stencilled curtain

In a crisp combination of blue and white, these curtains make a striking statement which belies their
simplicity. The feather motif is delicate, but, used with
a strong fabric colour, would not look out of place in
the kitchen, bathroom or bedroom. This is perhaps
the easiest of the projects included in this book, but a
particular favourite of mine. The beauty of the design
lies in its calm simplicity. Too many repeats of the
feather stencil and these curtains would become
fussy, quite the reverse of the look achieved here. By
placing the stencils carefully, using a light touch and
exercising some restraint, your aim should be to
achieve a calm, floating-feather look.

Close-up of one feather design.

ice poppies
bed linen

♥

Stamping on fabric is one of the easiest and most immediate ways in which to enliven and personalise bed linen. Choose quality white Egyptian cotton sheets, duvet cover and pillowcases. A good 100 percent cotton fibre will accept and fix the paint readily. It will also wash and wear well, giving you many years of use. For the stamp design, select a single small- to medium-sized motif – one that will sit easily with the furnishings in your room. Spend time and be careful in selecting the right motif as it will be with you for the life of the bed linen. The general rule for stamping of 'fewer is better' also applies to bedding. Avoid a pattern which is too busy: personalising linen is all about making you more content with your surroundings.

▶ 45

FABRIC

tablecloth and napkins

♥

The textures and colours of the seaside were my inspiration for this unusual tablesetting, perfect for al fresco dining on hot summer days. The mood is restful, and redolent of lazy days spent barefoot, combing the beach for shell souvenirs. I chose a natural sand-coloured linen to complement the shell motifs printed in a dark, maritime blue and white. Using a combination of stamping and stencilling techniques, as here, gives the design a characteristic fullness, and allows the details to be accentuated.

While closely woven fabric gives the clearest stencils, it is fun to experiment with the effects which can be achieved with different weaves and textures of fabric. In this instance, I was delighted with the way the fabric accepted the stamps and stencils: the slightly uneven effect adds another texture dimension.

Detail showing one shell stamp overlaid with a decorative stencil.

velvet stencilled cushion

♥

Comfort and good looks are the two major factors to consider when planning the soft furnishings of a room. Unfortunately, even the most elegant sofa can be disappointingly stiff and unyielding. This is where the humble cushion comes in. A couple of plumped-up cushions can make all the difference on such a sofa, and can turn a cold armchair into a cosy nest you will be reluctant to leave.

In addition to their ability to bring comfort, cushions are also a decorative nicety: they can add a splash of colour or bring together a daring mix of fabrics; they can blend in or make a strong statement. They can be firm or soft and squishy, large or small, and of course the variety of fabric and trimmings is endless: the decision is yours.

▶ 49

Choose any combination of stencils or one single motif to decorate the fabric surface.

I chose luxurious velvet in an old gold as the fabric for this stencilling project. Velvet is always irresistible – warm and soft to the touch, it feels gloriously extravagant, yet it is not vastly expensive, especially when you buy it in small, remnant-sized lengths.

The beauty of this design is in its subtlety. A scattering of small motifs stencilled on the velvet in clear fabric paint catch the light and create an interesting contrast in textures.

▶ 51

furniture

▶ 53

S tencilled painted furniture – along with stencilled wallpaper – reached a peak of popularity in the Europe of the 1800s. When the first settlers left for America, they took with them the technique of stencilling, and proceeded to decorate their rustic homes with remembered, much-loved designs.

Painted furniture is an ideal subject for stencilling and stamping, provided the surface is smooth and regular. Even the most tired piece of furniture can be improved with a lick of paint and the application of a stencil. Chairs, tables, linen boxes and chests of drawers are most commonly favoured with this kind of attention, but the list is almost inexhaustible: doors, kitchen cupboard doors, wardrobe doors, toyboxes, headboards, bathroom cabinets – even wooden bath panelling – all come to mind. Secure the stencil to prevent it shifting, keep the paint on the brush minimal, to prevent the paint from creeping, then even children can achieve satisfying results. Stamping requires a bit more skill, since the stamp needs to be placed accurately and cleanly for the best results, but stamping with potato, rubber or sponge on scrap paper and fabric is good practice.

The four projects selected for inclusion in this chapter satisfied the criteria of simple style, namely function, simplicity and style. A simple rectangular table is given a base coat in a neutral colour, and is transformed into a faux mosaic tile table which would freshen up any bathroom or conservatory. I chose blues, lilac and grey for my table, but fire or earth colours would be exciting

too. An ordinary upright chair, the sort that lurks in any large kitchen, is given a 'brass stud' finish with the clever use of a dot stamp, and a fleur de lys stamp design smartens up a dull blanket box. The stencilled chest of drawers – first lime washed before a pretty laurel leaf motif is applied – makes a charming addition to a romantic bedroom without being fussy.

FURNITURE

stamped
blanket box

♥

This blanket box was a perfect subject for stencilling or stamping. The straightforward design, with its simple lines and smooth rectangular surfaces, would have shown off to maximum effect any one of the stencil and stamp designs I considered. In the end, I teamed a traditional fleur de lys design, stamped in a formal pattern on each of the surfaces, with a contemporary, fresh colour scheme of yellow and sage green. A navy blue tassel picks up the colour of the fleur de lys and provides the finishing touch. The result has all the elements of simple style – simplicity, function and style – and I think you'll love it.

Classical motifs always work well. Keep the background colour scheme minimal to show the motif to best effect.

laurel leaf
chest of drawers

♥

A chest of drawers is probably one item of furniture which is common to all our homes, and which will outlive our decorating fads and fancies. The chest of drawers purchased for the arrival of the new baby and carefully packed with tiny garments will, some years later, stand with drawers half open, stuffed with baggy tracksuits and tee-shirts. Gone will be the Peter Rabbit-type nursery curtains and lampshade, replaced by posters of current sporting heroes and pop stars. But the chest of drawers need not be frozen in time. By stencilling on a design which reflects the age of the room's occupant, and which complements the decorative theme of the room, you can keep pace with evolving tastes without spending a fortune. This pretty chest of drawers, perfect for a feminine bedroom, was lime washed before a laurel leaf design was stencilled on to it.

► 59

Clean simple lines complement the laurel leaf pattern on the corner of this chest of drawers.

m o s a i c
t a b l e t o p

♥

Magnificent mosaic: whether a classical piece, gracing the floor of an ancient Venetian church, or a geometric design in the brightly-lit bathroom of a Las Vegas casino, mosaic is everywhere. This is an old and enduring art, loved as much for its vibrant colours as for its designs.

Here, I show you how you can create your own 'mosaic' tabletop using the simple technique of stamping, without the bother of glasscutting, grouting or specialist tools; all you need is a mosaic tile-sized stamp, acrylic paint – and a steady hand. In fact, perhaps the most difficult part about making this tabletop is deciding on the colours for your 'tiles'. I chose a fresh blue/grey/lilac scheme, which is perfect for the bathroom setting photographed, but for a different room, say a conservatory, I could have chosen a medley of greens, fire or earth colours.

Once you have mastered the technique of applying the paint to the stamp to give an authentic mottled look – reminiscent of traditional Italian glass tiles – you might like to experiment with a black and white scheme, or even a pattern.

62 ◄

upholstery
tack chair

A single straight-backed chair, the sort you might pull up to the kitchen table when you stop for a coffee break, is often the orphan of home decorating. Now you can give that boring old chair a spot of attention with this cunning idea. Using a dot stamp dipped in a rough blend of bronze and black paint to stamp rows of 'metallic' dots, you can create an apparently three-dimensional upholstery tack effect.

Once it has undergone its transformation, you won't want to tuck this chair behind the kitchen door out of sight; you'll want to find a place for it where it can be the focus of attention and admiration! In the hallway, perhaps, in the study, or maybe on the landing...?

Close-up of the 'metallic' dot pattern.

accessories

It is the small things, the little touches, which give any home its unique appeal. The way we attend to the fine details around the home says more about us than weeks of painstaking wallpapering or a designer kitchen ever could. Perhaps this is because it is here where the decorating 'buck' stops – these accessories, each carefully chosen from an often bewildering array of colours, styles and sizes, represent the very essence of our style. Simple style is all about eschewing unnecessary clutter; paring back to simple, uncomplicated lines; favouring natural materials and the celebration of space. This does not exclude the use of accessories; on the contrary, when

chosen and placed with care, accessories can enhance simple style through contrast, harmony and even humour. The technique of stencilling and stamping is an easy and effective way to person-alise your purchased finds and, should you later wish to make an identical copy of an earlier creation, the technique, by its definition, allows you do just that. My choice of projects includes ideas for those hand-me-down items that we are all given when we set up home, but which need a personal stamp to make them our own.

The stencilling and stamping beginner will find that accessories are a good place to start, since most of the items are small and the outlay modest. From a vast selection of possible projects, I have chosen four easy projects which are well within the reach of the novice: a glass bowl given star treatment; a pair of sophisticated 'gilt' picture frames; a lampshade with an intriguing spiral design and a set of striped storage jars and labels for your kitchen. I hope success with these small projects will fire your creative spark and perhaps encourage you to develop your own ideas; any one of these stencilling ideas can be adapted to suit your own taste and needs.

ACCESSORIES

frosted glass bowl

Glass is amazingly versatile. It can be cut, blown and moulded into the most intricate shapes; it may be clear or opaque, coloured or frosted; it can be functional or decorative, thick or thin. But, despite its potential, I suspect we all have some rather uninspiring glassware, possibly a vase or bowl, a jug, or even a set of glasses. In spite of its smooth surface, glass makes a very successful subject for stencils provided the stencil is taped down securely before you begin.

This bowl, stencilled with stars and filled with floating candles, makes a sparkling centre-piece for a special occasion, but it could just as well show off a wickedly tempting chocolate mousse or a festive selection of chocolates, nuts and dates. Deceptively simple to make, this bowl takes no more than an hour or two to complete.

▶ 71

Detail of a large frosted opaque star.

picture
frames

♥

A frame has the potential to 'make or break' a picture. The picture which will stop you in mid-stride when mounted in one frame may not get a second glance if mounted in another way. Choosing a frame can be a frustrating exercise: you have in mind a style or finish which apparently has yet to be invented, let alone manufactured, and your aching feet will vouch for your lack of success. What are your options? Learning the skill of picture framing is certainly one alternative, but may be more of a commitment than you are ready to make. Another alternative is to buy a ready-made frame with a simple design, and embellish it to suit yourself.

7 2 ◄

Black and gold frames look elegant and stylish without detracting from the focus of the picture.

These elegant frames draw attention to the small pictures within, but, more than that, they are themselves works of art which will attract many an admiring glance. Each was first painted with a base coat of black and then rubbed with a little gold gilt cream to enhance the pattern in relief. A border stencil was applied, first in black and then, moving the stencil slightly downwards, in gold paint, thus creating a drop shadow effect. This is a very easy, but most rewarding, project.

string stamped
lampshade

♥

The ambience of a room relies heavily on lighting. For mood lighting, it is often best to use individual lamps, or spot lights, and avoid the glare of general lighting. A lamp, placed nearby at the right height, can turn a comfortable chair into a favourite reading refuge, as well as a warm focus for the room.

When choosing a lampshade, make sure your shade width is in proportion to the height of the lamp-stand, to prevent a bottom-heavy or top-heavy look. Also, remember that the shape of the shade and its colour will affect the amount and intensity of the light it will provide.

I have made more of this textured lampshade by simply stamping a repeating spiral design in a rich yellow ochre around the base. Try experimenting with colour and texture, but bear in mind the silhouette effect on your design when the lamp is switched on.

storage jars and labels

♥

A glance inside my kitchen cupboards reveals a motley collection of unsightly jars, cartons, tins and bags containing coffee, tea, rice, sugar and flour. My spice cupboard is worse – spice bottles of different sizes jostle for space, some knocked down in the crush – and finding the spice required for a recipe involves unpacking the cupboard and examining the bottles one by one. A storage nightmare, and the inspiration for this project.

With a bit of imagination, a pot of bright enamel paint, a stamp and some stencils, I have turned the kitchen storage problem into an asset. Blue-and-white striped storage jars announce their contents in clear black lettering, and spice bottles with smart labels stand to attention in ordered rows. I think you will love these storage jars so much you'll want them on display, so bear that in mind when you choose your colour scheme!

putting it together

▶ 81

T he projects described in *Simple Style Stamps & Stencils* are all well within reach of the average reader. The designs are simple and the materials required couldn't be more basic – principally paint, brushes, masking tape and a mixture of stencils or stamps. The templates for the stencils and stamps are printed on pages 104–111. Ready-made stencils and stamps are widely available from the larger do-it-yourself stores and, increasingly, from specialist stencil/stamp shops, where staff will be able to answer your questions and offer advice.

Making a stencil involves the transfer of a design onto the stencil material. For this, the easiest method is to use a clear plastic stationery folder or clear acetate film, tracing paper or photocopied design, a craft knife and a cutting mat, preferably of the self-healing variety. For a large design, simply tape pieces of clear plastic together to the required length. With clear plastic you can see exactly where you are placing your stencil and it is easy to transfer your designs onto.

Trace the outline of your chosen design, or alternately photocopy your own choice of motif. Tape the image to the cutting mat so that it does not shift. Now secure the plastic on top. Holding the blade away from you, carefully cut out the stencil using a craft knife. It is important that you cut cleanly without breaching the design lines, as any irregularities will affect the clarity of your stencil. Don't forget to include strengthening 'bridges' if you are designing your own stencil.

Stamps are cut from foam or rubber which can then be glued to a block of wood for easy handling. Wood allows an even pressure to be applied when stamping. High density (condensed) rubber foam is good for detailed designs, while low density, synthetic foam, such as a bath sponge, gives a rougher result. When using condensed foam, trace designs off the source using tracing paper and then use spray adhesive to attach the tracing to the foam. Cut out using a craft knife. Low density foam is too soft for tracing purposes. Instead, draw freehand designs onto the foam using a water-based marker, then cut out using sharp scissors. Rinse out all traces of the marker pen.

The secret of stencilling and stamping is in the controlled use of paint. Always begin by pouring a little paint onto a plate. For stamping, use a small roller or a brush to apply paint to the stamp, then press the stamp firmly onto the required surface. For stencilling, dip the tip of the brush into the paint and blot off the excess on a cloth or paper towel. You should aim to have a brush which is almost dry. Hold the brush perpendicular to

the surface and, working away from the edges towards the centre of the stencil, apply the paint, building up the colour gradually. Stippling, or dabbing, flicking and rotating the brush all give different results. If paint bleeds under the edge of the stencil, you have used too much. Some people prefer to use oil-based paint sticks, which are 'drier' than paint, and some use sponges to apply the paint. Try out different methods on scrap paper first until you are comfortable with a technique that suits you. In general solvent-based paints are not recommended since they distort or melt stencil materials.

You will want to re-use a favourite stencil, and often stencils need to be reversed to achieve the inverse of the design, so it is vital to clean your stencils frequently and effectively. If you are covering large wall or floor surfaces, cut extra stencils before you begin, so that damaged or scratched stencils

can be discarded and replaced quickly without hindering the work in progress. Adequate preparation will always ensure better results and less wasted time. Wipe off water-based paint by soaking the plastic in warm soapy water. Clean your brushes after stencilling in warm, soapy water, then rinse and leave to dry. Once dry, use a loosely-tied elastic band to hold and keep the bristles in shape.

checked stamped floor

♥

Give your room a new look with this fresh floor design in the crocus colours of early spring.

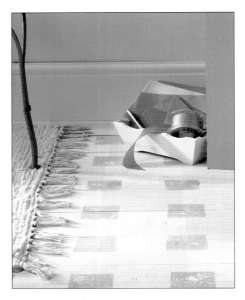

MATERIALS

Quantities given are for an average-sized room.

◆ *2.5 litres/³⁄4 gallon pale grey/mauve paint in eggshell finish for base coat*

◆ *1 litre/¹⁄4 gallon pale yellow paint in eggshell finish*

◆ *1 litre/¹⁄4 gallon cream paint in eggshell finish*

◆ *1 litre/¹⁄4 gallon lilac paint in eggshell finish*

◆ *1 litre/¹⁄4 gallon mauve paint in eggshell finish*

◆ *Four 2.5cm/1in brushes*

◆ *Two square stamps: one 10cm/4in, one 20cm/8in*

1 Remove flaking paint and old varnish from the wooden floorboard surface. Then sand, prime and give the floor an undercoat. Oil-based paints are best for floors as they are durable and therefore withstand heavy traffic.

2 For this floor, apply a liberal base coat of pale grey/mauve to the prepared floorboards.

3 Dab cream and pale yellow onto a large, square stamp without blending them too much.

4 Begin stamping the floor along the edge and, once you have completed one row, use the last stamp as a positioning guide.

5 Dab two colours (lilac and mauve) onto the smaller square stamp, taking care not to blend them too much.

6 Position over the intersection of the larger squares and print.

leaf stamped lime floor

♥

Create a truly contemporary appearance with limed floorboards stamped with a leaf design.

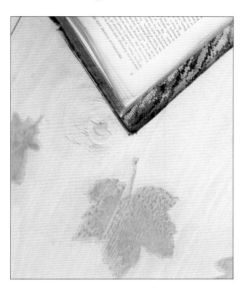

MATERIALS

Quantities given are suitable for an average-sized room.

◆ *1 litre/¼ gallon blue/grey paint with eggshell/satin finish for 'ageing' base coat*

◆ *1 litre/¼ gallon lime white paint with eggshell/satin finish*

◆ *Leaf-shaped stamps cut from foam rubber (see page 107)*

◆ *750ml/27fl.oz gloss varnish*

◆ *5cm/2in paint brush*

◆ *Paint kettle*

◆ *Cloth*

◆ *White spirit*

◆ *Container*

◆ *Small roller*

1 Prepare the floor as described on page 84, step 1. Age new floorboards like these with a base coat wash made from one part blue/grey paint mixed with three parts white spirit. Leave to dry thoroughly.

2 Pour a small amount of gloss varnish into a container. Pick up a small amount on the roller and apply an even coat to a leaf stamp.

3 To make a border around the room, apply different leaf stamps 15cm/6in away from the skirting board, changing the angle of each print as desired. Allow to dry thoroughly before proceeding to the next step.

4 Apply a lime wash made of one part lime white paint and four parts white spirit. Brush on evenly in the direction of the grain.

5 Once the wash has begun to soak into the wood, wipe over the stamps with a clean cloth. The leaf shapes will become visible as the paint dries.

green gingham floor

♥

This cool green gingham floor is perfect for a conservatory or kitchen – and it is surprisingly simple to do.

MATERIALS

Quantities given are for an average-sized room.

◆ *2.5 litres/³⁄4 gallon lime white paint in eggshell finish for base coat*
◆ *1 litre/¹⁄4 gallon mid-green paint in eggshell finish*
◆ *1 litre/¹⁄4 gallon darker green paint in eggshell finish*
◆ *Pencil and large ruler*
◆ *Stencil 30cm/12in square*
◆ *2.5cm/1in brush*

1 Prepare the floor as described on page 84 (checked stamped floor), step 1.

2 Apply a base coat in lime white eggshell paint.

3 The width of each plank will determine the size of the squares. Using a large ruler butted along the edge of each plank to achieve a sharp edge, stipple mid-green paint down the length of the plank. Repeat until all the stripes in one direction are complete.

4 Measure the width of the planks and, using these measurements, stipple mid-green paint across in the opposite direction to form a grid pattern.

5 Using a stencil cut to the size of the square at the intersections, stipple a square of darker green.

n a u t i c a l   r o p e   t w i s t   f l o o r

♥

Bring the tang of the sea and the creak of the wooden deck to your bathroom with this nautical floor decoration

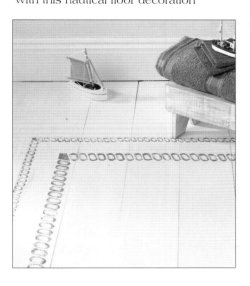

MATERIALS
Quantities given are suitable for an aver-age-sized room.
◆ *2.5 litres/¾ gallon white paint in eggshell finish for base coat*
◆ *250ml/9fl.oz dark blue paint in eggshell finish*
◆ *Pencil and ruler*
◆ *Masking tape*
◆ *Stencil brush*
◆ *Two rope twist stencils (see page 105)*
◆ *Paint brush*

1 Prepare the floor as described on page 84 (checked stamped floor), step 1.

2 Apply a base coat using white eggshell paint.

3 Using the pencil and ruler, draw a guideline around the edge of the floor.

4 Begin at a corner with the narrow rope twist stencil and stipple a little dark blue paint along the edge of the stencil to create a shade effect. Continue until the border is complete, apart from the corner gaps.

5 Now, working with the wider stencil and using the same technique, position and stencil a second border within the first and a small distance from it. Continue until the second border is complete, apart from the corner gaps.

6 Mask off the gaps in the corners with masking tape. Lightly stipple using the same blue paint.

spiral wall finish

♥

Scrolls and rosettes offer a classical appearance, emphasised by the cool blue and white colour scheme.

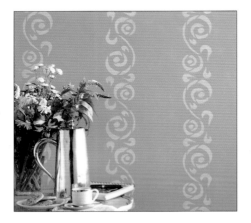

MATERIALS
Quantities given are suitable for an average-sized room.
◆ *2.5 litres/³⁄4 gallon powder blue matt emulsion for base coat*
◆ *1 litre/¹⁄4 gallon white matt emulsion*
◆ *Household sponge*
◆ *Stencil brush*
◆ *Stencil (see page 105)*
◆ *Masking tape and tape measure*
◆ *Pencil and spirit level*
◆ *Cloth*
◆ *Length of wood the height of the wall between the skirting board and cornice*

1 Remove any dirt, dust and flaking paint from the wall.

2 Dip one side of the household sponge into the powder blue matt emulsion. Wipe off the excess on the side of the can. To create a soft mottled paint effect, using the sponge, apply the emulsion onto the wall using a circular motion. Once dry, any uneven areas can be buffed over with a small amount of paint.

3 Working across the wall from left to right, mark points 30cm/12in apart.

4 Tape a spirit level to the wood and draw a vertical line through every marked point as a guide for the stencil.

5 Apply masking tape to each end of the stencil. Place the stencil at the top of the wall, aligning the top edge with the pencil line.

6 Dip the stencil brush into white emulsion and wipe off any excess onto a cloth or paper towel to prevent any paint creeping under the stencil. Apply the paint by stippling.

7 Peel the stencil away from the wall from the bottom upwards, to prevent any smearing. Alternate the design by turning the cleaned stencil upside down.

plaster spot wall finish

♥

This unusual paint and plaster application is quick to apply, fast-drying and creates a very effective finish for a plastered wall.

MATERIALS

Quantities given are suitable for an average-sized room.

◆ *2.5 litres/¾ gallon stone green matt emulsion*
◆ *2.5 litres/¾ gallon plaster white matt emulsion*
◆ *Powder interior filler*
◆ *Paintbrushes*
◆ *Small sponge roller*
◆ *Medium artist's brush*

1 Remove any dirt, dust and flaking paint from the wall.

2 Brush the wall with a base coat of green and allow to dry.

3 Apply a generous coat of plaster white matt emulsion over the green base coat in random, sweeping strokes. Do not cover the green entirely – the random appearance will create a rough plaster look.

4 Mix the plaster white emulsion paint with interior filler – one part emulsion to one part filler. Dab a small amount onto one end of the roller. Firmly press the roller onto the wall in the required position until the mixture is pushed out to the edges of the roller. Space plaster circles over the wall.

5 Rotate the tip of an artist's brush in a circular motion in the middle of the stamp to flatten any peaks in the mixture where the roller was pulled away from the wall. Allow to dry thoroughly.

♥

This sophisticated design is a remarkably simple, yet striking, example of the versatile art of stencilling. Applied in two stages, to build up the shadow effect, this stencil idea will give a wall a truly personal touch.

MATERIALS
Quantities given are suitable for an average-sized room.
◆ *2.5 litres/¾ gallon claret red emulsion*
◆ *Sample pot ultramarine blue acrylic paint*
◆ *Sample pot gold acrylic paint*
◆ *Sample pot silver acrylic paint*
◆ *Masking tape*
◆ *Three stencil brushes*
◆ *Two-layer monogram stencil (see pages 109–111)*

1 Remove any dirt, dust and flaking paint from the wall.

2 Apply a base coat of claret red emulsion to the wall surface.

3 Place the first layer of the stencil in position on the wall. Using a stencil brush, stipple in ultramarine blue paint.

4 Using a second brush, pick out the decorative leaves in gold. Allow to dry.

5 Carefully position the second layer of the stencil to fit over the first. Using silver paint, stencil the letter, then flick paint inwards from the end of each border line.

6 Stipple the decorative leaves in gold as before.

tulip wall panel

♥

Make much more of a special antique shop find, or give a dull alcove a treat with this unusual wall treatment.

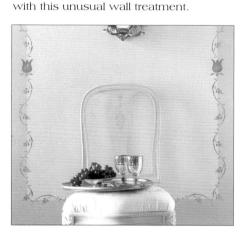

MATERIALS

Quantities given are suitable for an average-sized room.

◆ *2.5 litres/¾ gallon ice blue emulsion paint for the base coat*
◆ *1 litre/¼ gallon cream emulsion paint*
◆ *Sample pot sage green acrylic paint*
◆ *Sample pot pale green acrylic paint*
◆ *Sample pot dark red acrylic paint*
◆ *Tulip stencil and border (see page 108)*
◆ *Wallpaper paste*
◆ *Masking tape*
◆ *Three stencil brushes*
◆ *Spirit level*
◆ *Ruler*

1 Ensure that the surface is free of dirt and dust, and that any flaking paint has been removed. Emulsions, acrylics and stencil paints are all suitable for use on plaster walls.

2 Using a sponge, apply a base coat of ice blue emulsion to create a soft, mottled effect.

3 Using the spirit level and ruler, mark out the panel, taking care that its proportions balance with the room. Mask off the panel with masking tape.

4 Mix cream emulsion paint with wallpaper paste in a ratio of 1:1, and apply to the panel with a large brush in a vertical dragging motion.

5 Find the centre point of each side of the panel and stencil a tulip head over each mark. Make sure the tulip head remains upright on all four sides.

6 Working away from the tulip head, stencil the border first in one direction. Clean the stencil thoroughly, then flip it over in the other direction to produce the mirror image.

feather stencilled curtain

♥

Transform your plain curtains with this delicate feather motif – all you need is fabric paint, brushes and a stencil.

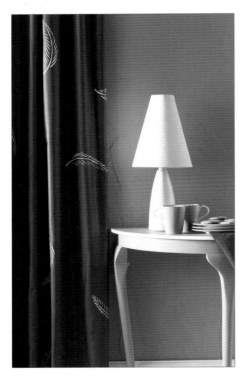

1 Wash and iron the curtains to remove any dressing and to allow for shrinkage.

2 Protect your working surface. Smooth out the fabric onto a table top and place a piece of cardboard under the area to be stencilled. Hold the fabric in place using strips of masking tape.

3 Hold the stencil in position and stipple with white fabric paint.

4 Using a second brush and pale blue paint, apply paint to the feather tips.

MATERIALS

Quantities given are suitable for one pair of curtains.

◆ *One pair of navy blue ready-made curtains*
◆ *Two small pots white fabric paint*
◆ *Small pot pale blue fabric paint*
◆ *Masking tape*
◆ *Cardboard*
◆ *Feather stencil (see page 108)*
◆ *Two stencil brushes*

92 ◄

ice poppies bed linen

♥

Cut your own floral pattern from a piece of foam to make an original stencil design, or choose a motif that will co-ordinate with wall coverings and window treatments.

MATERIALS

Quantities given are suitable for a single duvet cover and one pillowcase.

◆ *Single duvet cover and one pillow-case in white Egyptian cotton*
◆ *Two small pots pale blue fabric paint*
◆ *Small pot white fabric paint*
◆ *Small pot green fabric paint*
◆ *Flower-shaped stamp cut from foam rubber (see page 107)*
◆ *Small roller*
◆ *Cardboard*
◆ *Container*
◆ *Selection of artist's and stencil brushes*
◆ *Masking tape*

1 Iron the duvet cover and pillowcase. Place a piece of cardboard under the top layer of fabric to prevent the paint from printing onto the layer below.

2 Tape the edges of the pillowcase to the work surface to create a frame within which to print the stamps.

3 Pour a small quantity of light blue fabric paint into a container and, using a roller, apply a thin layer to the surface of the stamp.

4 Apply white paint to the flower centre using an artist's brush or stencil brush. Press the stamp firmly onto the fabric in the required position.

5 Repeating steps 3 and 4, randomly cover the surface of the pillowcase, allowing sufficient space between each for each flower stem.

6 With a fine artist's brush and green paint, paint the stem for each flower.

7 Complete the top surface of the duvet cover in the same way, but, for the underside, apply closely-spaced flower heads without stems.

t a b l e c l o t h   a n d   n a p k i n s

The colours, textures and images of the seaside were the inspiration for this table linen which combines the techniques of stamping and stencilling.

MATERIALS
Quantities given are approximate and depend on the size of the tablecloth and napkins.
- ◆ *Tablecloth and napkins in natural linen*
- ◆ *Small pot white fabric paint*
- ◆ *Small pot dark blue fabric paint*
- ◆ *Shell stamps and stencils (see page 109)*
- ◆ *Masking tape*
- ◆ *Cardboard*
- ◆ *Lining brush and stencil brush*
- ◆ *Small roller*
- ◆ *Palette*

1 Wash and iron the fabric to remove any dressing and to allow for shrinkage.

2 Smooth the fabric onto a flat surface and place a piece of cardboard under the area to be stamped.

3 Pour a little white fabric paint onto a palette and, using the roller, apply a good amount onto the shell stamp. Place the stamp in position at the corner of the fabric and stamp firmly. Stamp all four corners then position and stamp the border. Allow to dry.

4 Carefully place the shell stencil over the stamp. Dip the tip of the stencil brush in dark blue paint and flick inwards from the edge of the stencil. Do not cover the white completely.

5 Using a fine brush and dark blue paint, add a line of definition around each shell.

velvet stencilled cushions

♥

A scattering of small stencils in clear fabric paint emphasise the sumptuous textures of these velvet cushions. Choose a stencil design to complement your existing theme.

MATERIALS

Quantities given are suitable for at least two medium-sized cushions.

◆ *Pair of 'old gold' velvet cushions*
◆ *Medium pot clear fabric paint*
◆ *Stencil brush*
◆ *Stencil (see page 107)*
◆ *Masking tape*
◆ *Cardboard*
◆ *Selection of braids*
◆ *Template*

1 Make your template from the pattern provided on page 107.

2 Place a piece of cardboard inside the cushion cover to avoid printing through both layers of the fabric.

3 Secure the cushion cover by taping it to the work surface.

4 Position the stencil and stipple with clear fabric paint.

5 When stencilling at the edge, position the stencil so that it overlaps the side and then stipple as before.

6 Once the stencilling is complete and the paint is dry, sew on the braid.

stamped blanket box

♥

Choose a stencil motif and colour scheme to complement your room and turn a functional piece of furniture like this blanket box into a feature.

MATERIALS
Quantities given are approximate and depend on the size of the piece of furniture.
◆ *Blanket box or other suitable wooden box*
◆ *1 litre/¼ gallon sage green oil-based paint for the base coat*
◆ *250ml/9fl.oz dark yellow paint with eggshell finish*
◆ *Sample pot navy blue acrylic paint*
◆ *Fleur de lys stamp (see page 107)*
◆ *Small roller*
◆ *Lining brush*
◆ *2.5cm/1in brush*
◆ *Pencil and ruler*
◆ *Masking tape*

1 Sand off any flaking paint and old varnish from the surface. Apply a base coat of sage green paint.

2 Using a pencil and ruler, measure and draw a border with indented corners.

3 Mask off the area and dry brush dark yellow eggshell paint across the panel. Remove the masking tape carefully and immediately.

4 Lightly brush over the surface of the box with sage green, so that the yellow shows through.

5 Using the roller, apply navy blue paint to the stamp. Place the stamp in position at the corner and stamp firmly. Repeat at each corner.

6 Using a lining brush and blue paint, carefully add a blue line around the edge of each panel.

laurel leaf chest of drawers

♥

This fresh and feminine chest of drawers is no more than a weekend's work. Choose a simple motif like this laurel leaf and keep to one or two tones of the same colour for fuss-free results.

MATERIALS

Quantities given are approximate and depend on the size of the piece of furniture.

- ◆ Wooden chest of drawers
- ◆ 1 litre/¼ gallon lime white paint in eggshell finish for base coat
- ◆ 1 tube light green acrylic paint
- ◆ 1 tube mid-green acrylic paint
- ◆ Laurel leaf stencil (see page 106)
- ◆ 5cm/2in brush
- ◆ Pencil and ruler
- ◆ Masking tape

1 Sand off any flaking paint and old varnish from the surface. Using lime white paint as a base coat, dry brush each side of the chest of drawers in the direction of the grain.

2 Using a pencil and ruler, draw a centre line across the depth and width of each drawer as a guide for stencilling.

3 Position the leaf stencil. Using light green paint, flick the brush from the top of each leaf downwards.

4 With mid-green, stencil the stalk. Flick paint from the base of each leaf up.

5 Paint a border line in light green around the drawer front. Mask off the central leaf, position on each corner and stencil as before.

m o s a i c   t a b l e t o p

♥

Give a table a faux mosaic tile finish that is fresh, stylish and practical. This one looks stunning in the bathroom, but it would look just as good in the conservatory or kitchen. Experiment with colour and enjoy yourself!

MATERIALS

Quantities given are approximate and depend on the size of the furniture.
◆ *Small wooden table*
◆ *1 litre/¼ gallon pale beige oil-based paint for under coat*
◆ *1 tube lilac acrylic paint*
◆ *1 tube pale grey acrylic paint*
◆ *1 tube pale blue acrylic paint*
◆ *1 tube mid-blue acrylic paint*
◆ *Mosaic stamp (see page 106)*
◆ *Small brushes*
◆ *Varnish*
◆ *Cardboard*

1 Prepare the wood before you begin. Sand off any flaking paint and old varnish and apply an undercoat.

2 Apply a base coat of pale beige to the table top.

3 Dab several colours of acrylic paint onto a piece of cardboard, taking care not to blend them together too much.

4 Dip the stamp in the paint. Starting in one corner of the tabletop, press the stamp down firmly.

5 Using the previous stamp as a guide, continue across the tabletop, leaving a 'grout' line between each stamp.

6 For the edge, hold the top of the stamp at each end and print a line of 'tiles' along the side.

7 Apply a final protective coat of varnish if the area you are working on is to be used on a daily basis.

upholstery tack chair

♥

This simple straight-backed chair has been given a smart new look with this deceptively easy 'upholstery tack' stamp finish.

MATERIALS
Quantities given are approximate and depend on the size of the furniture.
- *Straight-backed wooden chair*
- *1 litre/¼ gallon dark turquoise oil-based paint for base coat*
- *1 tube black acrylic paint*
- *1 tube bronze acrylic paint*
- *1 tube light bronze acrylic paint*
- *1 tube gold relief paint*
- *Small brush*
- *Pencil and ruler*
- *1cm/⅓ in-diameter circle stamp*
- *Palette*

1 Prepare the wood as described on page 98, step 1. Apply a base coat of dark turquoise paint.

2 Draw a pencil guide line along the centre of each strut.

3 Pour black and bronze paint onto a palette, without blending the colours too much. Dab the stamp into the paint and begin stamping over the line. Proceed along the line, placing each stamp up against the one before, keeping the spacing tight.

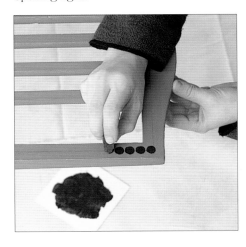

4 Using a small brush and light bronze paint, add a dot to each stamp.

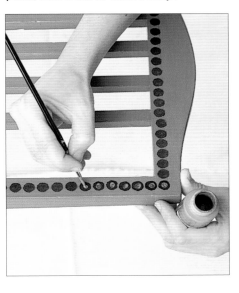

5 To add highlights, add a dot of gold relief paint straight from the tube, just off-centre over each stamp.

frosted glass bowl

♥

Floating candles illuminate this star-spangled bowl, making it a festive centre-piece for a celebration meal. When stencilling onto glassware, it is important to use glass paints, since normal emulsions and acrylics will not adhere and are therefore not suitable.

MATERIALS
- ◆ *Glass bowl of suitable design*
- ◆ *Small pot of frosting varnish*
- ◆ *Stencil brush*
- ◆ *Two star stencils: one large, one smaller (see page 107)*
- ◆ *Masking tape*
- ◆ *Soapy water*
- ◆ *Lint-free cloth*

1 Clean the glass thoroughly in warm soapy water and dry with a lint-free cloth.

2 Make sure the glass is completely dry and free from dust before you begin stencilling.

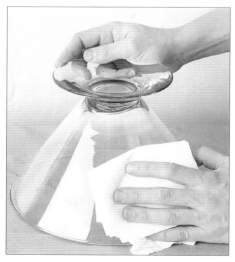

3 Tape the larger star stencil into position using masking tape. Stipple with frosting varnish. Repeat, spacing the large star at random around the bowl. Allow to dry.

4 Fill in any gaps as desired using the smaller star stencil.

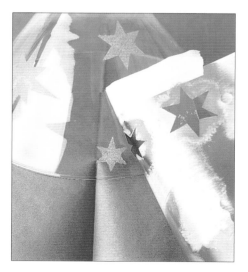

picture frames

♥

These simple frames have been given a metallic sheen and an interesting drop shadow border.

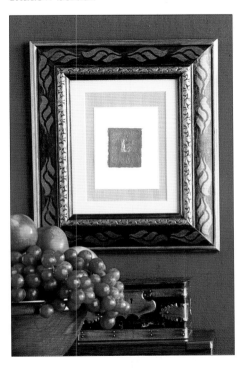

1 Paint the frame with black satin paint as a base coat. Allow to dry.

2 Rub a little gold gilt cream over the surface to leave a metallic sheen.

3 Tape the border stencil in position along the outer edge of the frame and stipple using black satin finish. Allow to dry.

4 Move the stencil slightly upwards. Stipple using gold acrylic paint. This will create a drop shadow effect.

MATERIALS

Quantities given are approximate and depend on the size of the frames.

◆ *Wooden picture frames*
◆ *250ml/9fl.oz black paint with satin finish for base coat*
◆ *Small pot gold gilt cream*
◆ *Small pot gold acrylic paint*
◆ *Masking tape*
◆ *Border stencil (see page 106)*
◆ *Two stencil brushes*
◆ *2.5cm/1in brush*

string stamped lampshade

♥

Design and make your own unique stamp for this lampshade project. Here, the string stamp complements the texture of the lampshade fabric, but you can adapt the design to suit your own requirements.

MATERIALS

Quantities given are suitable for a medium-sized lampshade.

◆ *Burgundy self-coloured lampshade*
◆ *Sample pot yellow ochre acrylic paint*
◆ *Cardboard*
◆ *Glue*
◆ *Pencil*
◆ *String*
◆ *Small roller*

1 Draw a scroll shape onto a small square of cardboard (see page 107).

2 Pipe glue over the pencil guideline.

3 Starting in the centre, curl a length of string around the glue scroll, pressing

the string into the glue as you work. Cut off the excess. Allow the stamp to dry.

4 Using a small roller, apply yellow ochre paint to the stamp.

5 Carefully stamp onto the lower edge of the lampshade. Repeat until the border detail is complete.

storage jars and labels

♥

Adapt this attractive storage solution to suit the colour scheme of your kitchen. When stencilling onto ceramicware, it is important to use enamel paints, since normal emulsions and acrylics will not adhere and are therefore not suitable.

MATERIALS

Quantities given are approximate and depend on the size and number of jars and labels.

- *Selection of storage and spice jars*
- *Sample pot navy blue enamel paint*
- *250ml/9fl.oz mid-blue enamel paint*
- *Small pot black enamel paint*
- *Label stamp (see page 104)*
- *2.5cm/1in-wide masking tape*
- *Lettering stencil (see page 104)*
- *Stencil brush and small roller*
- *White self-adhesive labels to fit spice jars*

1 For the labels, using the roller, apply navy blue paint to the label stamp. Print onto the self-adhesive labels.

2 Cut out along the outside edge of the blue border.

3 For the storage jars, fix masking tape in horizontal bands around each jar, allowing a 2.5cm/1in gap of white between the bands of tape.

4 Paint the gaps between masking tape bands in mid-blue enamel paint. Paint in the direction of the tape – using horizontal brush strokes. Completely cover any white areas. Allow to dry.

5 Place the lettering stencil in position and stipple in black enamel paint.

ABCDEFG
HIJKLMN
OPQRSTU
VWXYZ

104 ◀

stencil

storage jars and labels
Actual size

stamp

nautical
rope twist
floor stencil
Actual size

spiral wall finish stencil
Enlarge to 120%

laurel leaf chest of
drawers stencil
Actual size
**Reverse the image at the
broken line**

mosaic
tabletop
stamp
Actual size

picture frames stencil
Actual size
Reverse the image at the broken line

leaf stamped floor
Actual size

ice poppies bed linen stamp
Actual size

frosted glass bowl stencil
Actual size

velvet
stencilled
cushion
Actual size

stamped blanket box
Actual size

string stamped lampshade
Actual size

tulip wall panel
stencils
Actual size

feather
stencilled curtain
Actual size

tablecloth and napkins
Actual size. The stamp is defined by the blue line.
The stencil is defined by the black lines

First layer

initial letter monogram stencil
Actual size

Second layer

For the remaining initials see pages 110–111 and
enlarge them on a photocopier to 250%

index